D0820441

FEB   2016

UNSOLVED MYSTERIES

CROP CIRCLES

BY EMILY O'KEEFE

ABOUT THE AUTHOR

Emily O'Keefe is a writer and editor in Illinois. She has authored many stories and lessons for young people. O'Keefe has fond memories of visiting her grandmother's farm and would like to see a crop circle someday.

Published by The Child's World®
1980 Lookout Drive • Mankato, MN 56003-1705
800-599-READ • www.childsworld.com

ACKNOWLEDGMENTS
The Child's World®: Mary Berendes, Publishing Director
Red Line Editorial: Editorial direction
The Design Lab: Design
Amnet: Production

DESIGN ELEMENT: Shutterstock Images

PHOTOGRAPHS ©: iStock/Thinkstock, cover; iStockphoto, 5; Digital Vision/
Thinkstock, 7, 23; David Evison/Shutterstock Images, 8; Marcel Jancovic/
Shutterstock Images, 11; Moore Mike/Mirrorpix/Newscom, 12; Shutterstock
Images, 16; Jeff Tuttle/Butterfinger/AP Images, 18; Bob Collier/Press
Association/AP Images, 19; Lucy Pringle/Solent News/Rex Features/
AP Images, 21

ISBN 9781634070690
LCCN 2014959759

Printed in the United States of America
Mankato, MN
July, 2015
PA02266

TABLE OF CONTENTS

MYSTERY ON THE FARMS

In August 1980, a mysterious event happened in Wiltshire, England. A farmer discovered an odd sight in his oat fields. Someone—or something—had flattened much of the crop. These flattened areas formed three circles. He measured the circles. Each was about 60 feet (18 m) wide.

Farmers marveled at the pattern. No one knew who or what had made the circles. The shapes simply appeared overnight. Amazingly, the crops were barely harmed. The stalks were bent but not broken. They would continue to grow.

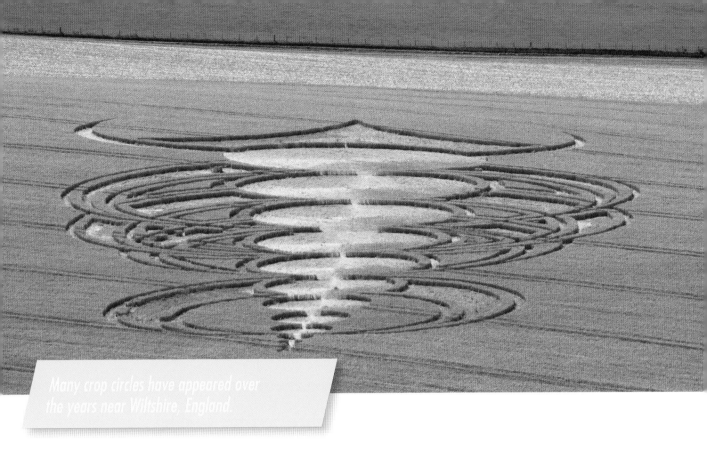

Many crop circles have appeared over the years near Wiltshire, England.

A newspaper reported on the mystery. Television shows told the strange story. Farmers across England responded. Many had seen similar patterns in their fields. Each time, the circles showed up overnight.

The next year, more patterns appeared on farms. People called them crop circles or crop formations. Soon, they appeared in other countries. Many were beautiful and eerie. Some people heard humming before the circles appeared. Others heard only silence. The circle makers vanished without a trace.

How Did the Circles Get There?

Scientists tried to solve the mystery. One important researcher was Terence Meaden. He studied more than 1,000 crop circles. Meaden thought that wind formed the circles. A sudden wind could swirl crops into a pattern.

Others disagreed. They said that the patterns were too complicated. Someone had made them on purpose.

Perhaps people made the crop circles. The circles were in places that people could enter easily. Some were too large for one person to make. But a group of people could work together. The group might make the circles after dark. They would have to be careful not to leave footprints.

Yet the crop circles appeared very quickly. No one noticed loud noises in the fields. Some experts doubted that people could be so quick or quiet. The shapes were also very exact. Could people really make them?

Author Richard Lawrence had a different **theory**. He said that aliens were visiting Earth. Crop circles were their messages for humans. Many people believed this idea. They wondered what the messages meant.

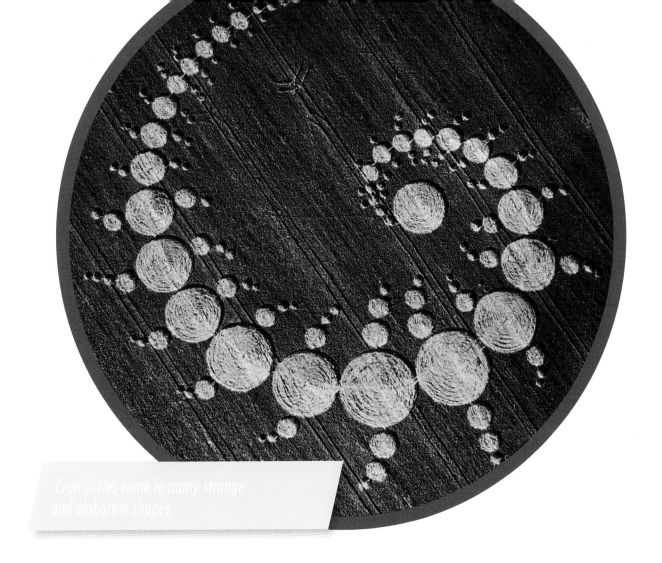

Crop circles come in many strange
and elaborate shapes.

Aliens might have special tools. Or they might be very

intelligent. Perhaps they could make crop circles quickly.

The strange patterns seemed to be from another world. But

there was no proof that aliens made them. No one even

knows if aliens exist.

Many thought that crop circles were linked to the mystery of Stonehenge.

New Circles

From 1980 to 1990, new crop circles appeared every year. They became more complicated. People visited the beautiful sights. Some farmers were proud of crop circles in their fields. They welcomed the visitors.

Often, the crop circles appeared near ancient **sacred** sites. Many were close to Stonehenge, a very old monument in England that is made of giant stones. Many mysteries remain about who built Stonehenge and how they built it. Crop circles have the same kind of mystery.

Scientists studied the new circles. One group of people camped out at a farm overnight. They wanted to catch whoever made the circles. The campers' attempt failed. A circle appeared nearby in the morning. But they did not see who had made it.

In 1990, 150 researchers gathered to discuss crop circles. That year, people spotted more than 900 circles. They still could not solve the mystery. People had ideas, but no proof.

The next year, everything changed. Two men announced that they had made the crop circles. It was a new twist in the mystery of the crop circles. But the mystery was far from over.

MYTH OR FACT?

Crop formations are always circles.

It is a myth that all crop patterns have the same shape. The first crop patterns were circles. Over time, other shapes appeared. Some crop formations are squares or lines. One looks like a jellyfish. Most are still circles, though. This is why people use the name "crop circles."

CHAPTER TWO

CROP CIRCLE ARTISTS

In 1978, Doug Bower and Dave Chorley lived in Hampshire, England. They shared a love of painting. Sometimes they made art together. One weekend, they created a new kind of art project: a crop circle.

The crop circle was Bower's idea. He had heard stories about aliens and UFOs. Bower was **skeptical** about these stories. He wanted to make a crop circle as a joke. It might trick people into thinking aliens had landed nearby. Bower had another reason for making the circle, too. He wanted to create a

Crop circles like this one in Slovakia appeared all around the world.

beautiful picture in the fields. Chorley agreed with this idea. He said they could use the land as a **canvas**.

The two men began making crop circles every week. They mastered more complex patterns. News stories reported their creations. Their plan was a success. No one knew their secret. Some thought aliens had made their circles.

Bower and Chorley laughed at these stories. But eventually they thought the joke had gone far enough. They decided to admit the truth.

How They Did It

In September 1991, Bower and Chorley talked to a reporter. They explained how they had made crop circles for 13 years. In the story, the reporter called them the "men who **conned** the world."

Bower and Chorley explained how they did it. First, they drew a picture of the design. Then, they went to the fields at night. The friends were quiet and careful. They stepped only

Doug Bower demonstrates his method for making crop circles using a plank and rope.

in existing tracks in the fields. That way, they did not leave footprints. They measured the area where they would make the circle.

Bower and Chorley used simple tools. They attached a 4-foot (1.2-m) board to a length of rope. The other end of the rope was anchored to the center of the circle. This method helps make a perfect circle. The men set the board flat on the ground and stepped on it to flatten the crops underneath. They did this all the way around the center point until a perfect circle was made. They stepped gently to avoid destroying the stalks. They repeated this process to finish their design.

The Crop Circle Test

Soon, the friends were famous. Dozens of people tried making crop circles themselves. Farmers and crop experts reacted to the news.

Many scientists decided that most or all crop circles were man-made. Terence Meaden had thought that the wind created crop circles. Bower's and Chorley's **confession** changed his mind. He decided that nature created only a small number of crop circles. The rest were **hoaxes**.

MYTH OR FACT?

It is a fact that people can make crop circles quickly. Bower and Chorley demonstrated making crop circles in a few hours. Other circle makers often take two to four hours for each design. Complex patterns take longer. One design included more than 100 circles. A team completed it in just six hours.

Some **cereologists** who studied the crop circles disagreed. They doubted that people could create such complex designs. Bower and Chorley agreed to a test. A reporter watched them make a crop circle. Then the reporter showed the circle to Pat Delgado. Delgado was an author and engineer. He had written a book about crop circles. He thought they could not be explained.

The crop circle fooled Delgado. "No human could have done this," he said. But humans had. The reporter told Delgado what he had seen. Delgado had to admit that he was mistaken.

Bower and Chorley proved that people could make crop circles. But the mystery was not entirely solved. Some crop circles remained hard to explain.

BELIEVERS, DOUBTERS, AND ARTISTS

After 1991, people looked at crop circles differently. Doug Bower and Dave Chorley said they made more than 200 circles. Most likely, they had created the first reported crop circles in Wiltshire. Yet some questions remained. There were thousands of crop circles all over the world. Who made the other circles?

For many scientists, the answer was easy. They concluded that humans made all or most crop circles. They knew that people could make crop

Many believe that aliens make some crop circles.

formations quickly. Perhaps Bower and Chorley were not the only circle makers between 1978 and 1991. Stories about their creations could have inspired others.

Another group of people still thought that crop circles were unexplained. These people were sometimes called crop circle believers. They described feeling bursts of energy when standing inside some crop circles. Some thought that the circles could heal injuries. Man-made crop circles would not have this effect.

In 1999, even Bower said that some crop circles were unexplained. He described seeing a UFO while making a crop circle. This sight convinced him that aliens might exist. The **origin** of some crop circles could be **extraterrestrial**.

Crop Circles Today

Crop circles have remained popular. People have found at least 12,000 of them. The formations are found in many countries. But most still appear in southern England. Many visitors come to tour the sites.

A large number of people today think crop circles are unexplained. They have different ideas about the origin of the circles. Some say that aliens make them. Others say that nature creates the circles. Either way, certain people agree that the circles are a message to humans. Yet no one knows what the message means. Some appear to contain numbers in Braille or binary code.

Believers know that people make some crop formations. But they think there is a difference between "real" and "hoax" crop circles. Many say that man-made circles are more harmful to crops.

Groups of believers search for crop circles. These groups study samples from the fields. They say that the circles make them feel connected to Earth. Other people join together to make new crop circles. They follow the process Bower and Chorley used.

Despite their name, crop circles can have various shapes and designs.

Like Bower and Chorley, many circle makers are artists. Some make crop formations as a joke. Others believe that they are a beautiful art form. Their designs include snowflakes and animals. One group even made a crop formation

This idea is a myth. Visitors sometimes bring pets to crop circles. A few people's dogs and cats became nervous or sick inside crop circles. Some people thought the animals sensed traces of aliens. But no one has proven that the crop circles caused the animals' reaction. Many animals behave normally in crop circles.

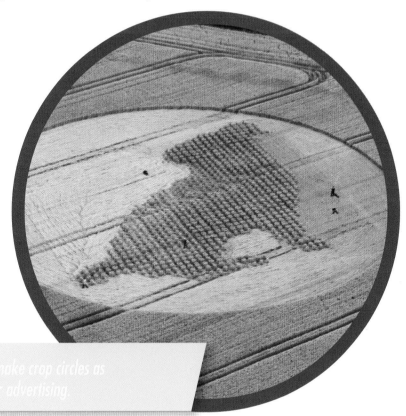

Some people make crop circles as a form of art or advertising.

MYTH OR FACT?

This is a fact. The earliest story is from a **pamphlet** from 1678. The author described a strange pattern found in a field of crops. The pamphlet contained an illustration of the pattern. The pattern looks similar to modern crop circles. But experts do not know if crop circles really existed in 1678. The author may have made up the story. Or people could have made the crop circles then like they do today.

shaped like a dentist's drill. Companies use crop circles to advertise. They hire circle makers to create pictures in the fields.

Crop circle artists still keep secrets. They do not identify which circles they make. They often work late at night. Some ask farmers for permission to use their fields. Others simply sneak in.

Artists and believers are similar in some ways. They like the mystery of crop circles. Artists try to keep that sense of mystery. Experts agree that people make at least some crop circles. But often they do not know which people have made them.

Each new crop circle adds to the mystery. The artists could be people who sneak into fields at night. Or they could be someone—or something—else entirely.

Many crop circles and their fantastic designs remain unexplained.

Glossary

canvas (KAN-vuss) A canvas is a stiff piece of material used for paintings. Crop circle makers compared farm fields to a giant canvas.

cereologists (sear-ee-AH-low-jists) Cereologists are people who study crop circles. Many cereologists gather samples from farms with crop formations.

confession (kon-FEH-shun) A person makes a confession by admitting to a secret. Doug Bower and Dave Chorley made a confession that they had created crop circles.

conned (KAHND) When people tell lies or play tricks, they have conned others. Crop circle makers conned people into thinking the circles were from aliens or UFOs.

extraterrestrial (ek-struh-tuh-RES-tree-ul) An extraterrestrial creature or thing is from outer space. Some people believe that extraterrestrial beings made the crop circles.

hoaxes (HOKE-ses) Hoaxes are jokes or tricks. Many people create crop circles as hoaxes to make others believe in aliens.

origin (OR-i-jin) An origin is where something comes from. The origin of many crop circles is still a mystery.

pamphlet (PAM-flet) A pamphlet is a small, short book. An old pamphlet showed a possible ancient crop circle.

sacred (SAY-kred) When something is sacred, people honor or value it. Crop circles have been found near sacred places such as old monuments.

skeptical (SKEP-ti-kul) A skeptical person doubts an idea. Some scientists are skeptical of the idea that aliens made crop circles.

theory (THEER-ee) A theory is an idea or explanation. One scientist had the theory that wind created crop circles.

To Learn More

BOOKS

Burns, Jan. *Crop Circles*. Detroit: KidHaven Press, 2008.

Duncan, John. *UFOs: The Unexplained*. Costa Mesa, CA:
Saddleback Educational Publishing, 2009.

Lunde, Paul. *The Secrets of Codes: Understanding the World of
Hidden Messages*. San Francisco: Weldon Owen, 2012.

WEB SITES

Visit our Web site for links about crop circles: **childsworld.com/links**

*Note to Parents, Teachers, and Librarians: We routinely verify our Web links to make sure
they are safe and active sites. So encourage your readers to check them out!*

Index